Table of Contents

Chris Pratt plays
a dinosaur trainer in
Jurassic World (2015).

INSPIRE

CHRIS PRATT

BY MARY BLECKWEHL

AMICUS LEARNING

Inspire is published by
Amicus Learning, an imprint of Amicus
P.O. Box 227
Mankato, MN 56002
www.amicuspublishing.us

Editor: Ana Brauer
Series Designer: Kathleen Petelinsek
Book Designer and Photo Researcher: Emily Dietz

Library of Congress Cataloging-in-Publication Data
Names: Bleckwehl, Mary E., author.
Title: Chris Pratt / by Mary Bleckwehl.
Description: Mankato : Amicus Learning, 2025. | Series: Inspire | Includes bibliographical references and index. | Audience: Ages 5–9 | Audience: Grades 2–3 | Summary: "Learn about movie star Chris Pratt and how he paved his way to Hollywood in this biography packed with photos and fact-filled text suitable for young readers. Includes a table of contents, glossary, further resources, and index" — Provided by publisher.
Identifiers: LCCN 2024012081 (print) | LCCN 2024012082 (ebook) | ISBN 9798892001038 (library binding) | ISBN 9798892001618 (paperback) | ISBN 9798892002196 (ebook)
Subjects: LCSH: Pratt, Chris, 1979—Juvenile literature. | Actors—United States—Biography—Juvenile literature. | Motion picture actors and actresses—Biography—Juvenile literature. | LCGFT: Biographies.
Classification: LCC PN2287.P66 B54 2025 (print) | LCC PN2287.P66 (ebook) | DDC 791.4302/8092 [B]—dc23/eng/20240327
LC record available at https://lccn.loc.gov/2024012081
LC ebook record available at https://lccn.loc.gov/2024012082

Photo Credits: Alamy Stock Photo/Album, 11, 12, ARCHIVIO GBB, 7, TCD Prod.DB, 15, Universal Pictures, 4; Associated Press/Alex J. Berliner, cover; Getty Images/ Astrid Stawiarz, 20, Axelle Bauer-Griffin, 21, Leon Bennett, 19, Noam Galai, 14; Shutterstock/Bohbeh, 13, Brostock, 17, Featureflash Photo Agency, 8, Kathy Hutchins, 16, Robert Biedermann, 9

Printed in China

Megastar

Chris Pratt waits on the movie set. A man falls into the dinosaur pen. Pratt rushes in to help. His voice calms the velociraptor. The man escapes.

None of it is real. But it's Pratt's job to make it look real. It's what actors do. Chris Pratt is an American television and movie actor.

Growing Up

Pratt was born in Virginia, Minnesota. When he was young, his family moved to Lake Stevens, Washington. In high school, he acted in his first play. He was a good athlete too. Pratt says that playing football helped prepare him for his acting career.

Pratt graduated
high school in 1997.

Pratt started his acting career in 2001.

Finding His Way

After high school, Pratt didn't know what he wanted to do. He acted in dinner theatres and took college classes. He tried many jobs. One was doing stand-up comedy. A friend invited him to Hawaii. He decided to go.

DID YOU KNOW?
Pratt was homeless in Hawaii. He lived in a Scooby-Doo van and a tent on the beach.

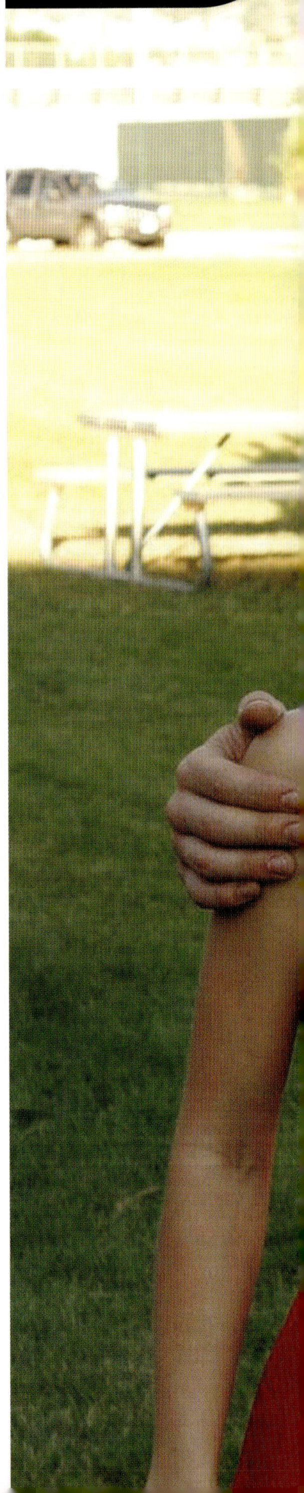

Pratt's first regular TV role was on the show *Everwood* (2002). He played a high school football player.

A Lucky Break

In Hawaii, Pratt got a job waiting tables. One day, he met an actress. She **recruited** him to be in a movie. This was his big chance. He said yes and moved to Los Angeles. The experience helped Pratt decide to be an actor.

PROPERTY OF
PC
EAK COUNTY
OTBALL
Everwoo

In an episode of *Parks and Recreation*, Pratt's character catches a possum. He later sings it a short song.

Breakthrough Role

In 2009, Pratt landed another TV role. It was a **temporary** part on the show *Parks and Recreation*. He played a lovable musician. Fans thought he was funny. His acting earned him a **permanent** part on the show. It skyrocketed his career.

THE AWESOME ALBUM

In *Parks and Recreation*, Pratt played in the *Mouse Rat* band. They later made a real album.

Blockbuster Years

In 2014, Pratt landed his first lead roles. He voiced Emmet in *The Lego Movie*. He starred as Star-Lord in *Guardians of the Galaxy*. In 2015, Pratt starred in the first *Jurassic World* movie. He returned for two other movies in the series. Chris Pratt was officially an action hero!

Who was the voice of Mario in *The Super Mario Bros. Movie* in 2023? Chris Pratt, of course!

Pratt played Star-Lord in all three of the *Guardians of the Galaxy* movies.

Pratt quickly rose to fame and became a household name.

A Hollywood Star

A good actor can play many different roles. Pratt has starred as a funny singer. He was a space hero. Pratt has won awards for his many roles. On April 21, 2017, Pratt received a star on the Hollywood Walk of Fame.

SWEATING THE PART

Pratt had to lose 60 pounds (27 kilograms) to play Star-Lord in *Guardians of the Galaxy*.

Family

Pratt is married and has three children. Their home is in Los Angeles. Sometimes they visit his farm in Washington. He has cattle and sheep there. Pratt enjoys the outdoors and time to relax.

Pratt poses with his wife, Katherine, at an event for *The Super Mario Bros. Movie*.

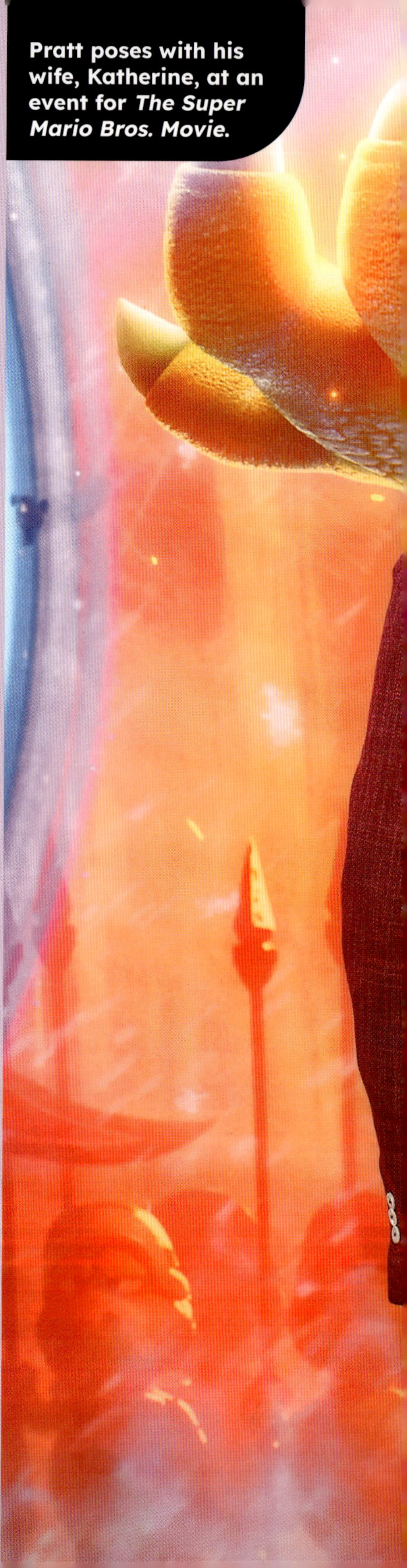

Pratt visits Ronald McDonald Houses. He hands out gifts to the children staying there.

Beyond the Screen

Pratt helps many **charities**. One is a teen center in his hometown of Lake Stevens, Washington. It is named for his father. Another gives glasses to needy children. His gift was inspired by his son, Jack. Jack was born with vision problems.

Pratt's son Jack inspires his charity work.

SUPER STATS

CHRIS PRATT

Born: June 21, 1979

Hometown: Lake Stevens, Washington

Birthplace: Virginia, Minnesota

Children: 3

TV Roles: *Everwood* (2002–2006), *Parks and Recreation* (2009–2015), *The Terminal List* (2022–)

Main Movie Roles: *The Lego Movie* (2014), *Guardians of the Galaxy* movies (2015, 2017, 2023), *Jurassic World* movies (2015, 2018, 2022), *The Super Mario Bros. Movie* (2023), *The Garfield Movie* (2024)

AWARDS

Saturn Award – Best Actor: 2015

Teen Choice Awards: 2017, 2018

Kids' Choice Awards: 2019

GLOSSARY

charities Groups that help people in need.

permanent Lasting a long time.

recruit To get someone to join.

temporary Lasting a short time.

READ MORE

Abdo, Kenny. **Chris Pratt.** North Mankato, MN: ABDO, 2019.

Kawa, Katie. **Chris Pratt Is Star-Lord.** Gareth Stevens Publishing, 2020.

London, Martha. **Chris Pratt.** Lake Elmo, MN: Red Line Editorial, 2020.

ON THE WEB

Britannica
https://www.britannica.com/biography/Chris-Pratt

Kiddle
https://kids.kiddle.co/Chris_Pratt

KidzSearch Wiki
https://wiki.kidzsearch.com/wiki/Chris_Pratt

INDEX

About the Author

Mary Bleckwehl is a children's author who loves cookie dough and talking to kids. She is happiest when she is biking and exploring new places. Mary lives in Minnesota with her husband and monster dog. Check out her books at marybleckwehl.com.